IT'S MY STATE!

VERMONT

Margaret Dornfeld

William McGeveran

Marshall Cavendish
Benchmark
New York

Published by Marshall Cavendish Benchmark
An imprint of Marshall Cavendish Corporation

Other Marshall Cavendish Offices:
Marshall Cavendish International (Asia) Private Limited, 1 New Industrial Road, Singapore 536196 •
Marshall Cavendish International (Thailand) Co Ltd. 253 Asoke, 12th Flr, Sukhumvit 21 Road, Klongtoey Nua,
Wattana, Bangkok 10110, Thailand • Marshall Cavendish (Malaysia) Sdn Bhd, Times Subang, Lot 46, Subang
Hi-Tech Industrial Park, Batu Tiga, 40000 Shah Alam, Selangor Darul Ehsan, Malaysia

Marshall Cavendish is a trademark of Times Publishing Limited

All websites were available and accurate when this book was sent to press.

Library of Congress Cataloging-in-Publication Data
        Dornfeld, Margaret.
        Vermont / Margaret Dornfeld, William McGeveran. — 2nd ed.
            p. cm. — (It's my state!)
        Includes bibliographical references and index.
        Summary: "Surveys the history, geography, government, economy, and people of Vermont"—Provided by publisher.
        ISBN 978-1-60870-660-0 (print) — ISBN 978-1-60870-815-4 (ebook)
        1. Vermont—Juvenile literature. I. McGeveran, William. II. Title. III. Series.
      F49.3.D67 2013
      974.3—dc23   2011020731

Second Edition developed for Marshall Cavendish Benchmark by RJF Publishing LLC (www.RJFpublishing.com)
Series Designer, Second Edition: Tammy West/Westgraphix LLC
Editor, Second Edition: Emily Dolbear

All maps, illustrations, and graphics © Marshall Cavendish Corporation. Maps and artwork on pages 6, 48, 49, 75, 76, and back cover by Christopher Santoro. Map and graphics on pages 9 and 41 by Westgraphix LLC.

The photographs in this book are used by permission and through the courtesy of:
Front cover: Vernon Siql/Superstock and Exactostock/Superstock (inset).
Alamy: Robert Shantz, 4 (left); NHPA, Joanne Pearson, 10; Science Photo Library, 16; Sandy Macys, 18 (top); Tom Uhlman, 20 (left); Andre Jenny, 20 (right); Eric Carr, 21; Gabe Palmer, 22; North Wind Picture Archives, 25; dbimages, 29; Rob Crandall, 36; John Elk III, 38; Peter Arnold Inc., 42; George Robinson, 43; Pat & Chuck Blackley, 52; Balfour Studios, 53; Daniel Dempster Photography, 62; Danny Hooks, 68; Nik Wheeler, 69. **Associated Press:** Associated Press, 12, 18 (bottom), 19, 31, 40, 44 (bottom), 45 (bottom), 47, 58, 60, 74. **Corbis:** Corbis, 35; Farrell Grehan, 66. **Getty Images:** Wire Images, 45 (left). **North Wind Picture Archives:** 44 (top). **Superstock:** age fotostock, 4 (right); 11, 56, 67; NHPA, 5 (left); 8; All Canada Photos, 5 (right); Visions of America, 14, 28, 64, 70; Anthony Butera, 15; IndexStock, 17, 50, 51; Photononstop, 26; Superstock, 33; The Art Archive, 34 (top right); Universal Images Group, 34 (left); Belinda Images, 54; Lucidio Studio, Inc., 71 (top); H. Stanley Johnson, 71 (bottom); Dale Jorgenson, 73.

Printed in Malaysia (T).
135642

VERMONT

CONTENTS

THE GREEN MOUNTAIN STATE

State Animal: Morgan Horse

In 1791, Justin Morgan, a Vermont teacher, became the owner of a young stallion named Figure. The horse was small but strong and fast. Figure became the father of a new breed, the Morgan, which is still known today for its athletic ability.

State Bird: Hermit Thrush

With its brown back and speckled breast, the hermit thrush can be hard to spot in the Vermont woods. It is better known for its flutelike song, which can be heard on summer days from just before dawn to sunset.

State Butterfly: Monarch

In 1987, a fifth-grade class in Cornwall suggested naming the monarch as the official state butterfly, and the state legislature agreed. The monarch, native to Vermont, is a familiar sight in late summer and early fall. The students said its colors recall many sides of Vermont: orange for autumn leaves, black for soil, white for snow, and yellow for fields of dandelions.

State Tree: Sugar Maple

American Indians taught the early European settlers the best way to get sap from sugar maples. Vermonters have been collecting sap—or tapping maple trees—ever since. The sap is often boiled to make syrup, but the process is slow. It takes about 40 gallons (150 liters) of sap to make a single gallon (3.8 l) of pure maple syrup.

State Fossil: White Whale

In 1849, workers building a railroad between Rutland and Burlington uncovered the fossil of a white whale. It had lived some 12,500 years earlier, when waters from the Atlantic Ocean covered that low-lying region. This white whale was named the state fossil in 1993.

State Amphibian: Northern Leopard Frog

Northern leopard frogs, also known as meadow or grass frogs, live in Vermont's ponds and wetlands. They have spots all over their green or brown bodies. Lawmakers made the northern leopard frog a state symbol in 1998, noting that its numbers were declining because of habitat loss and possible damage to its environment.

The Green Mountain State

Vermont is known for its quiet woods, deep snow, and shining waters. It can bring to mind a winding road, a covered bridge, a white church, or an old-fashioned country store. But more than anything else, Vermont means mountains.

The Green Mountains spread down the length of Vermont, forming a backdrop to the roadways and villages. The mountains light up with color in autumn, while in winter they cast evening shadows over snow-covered hills. They carry rivers and streams that help keep the landscape green. And they help give the state its scenic appeal. Vermont is known as the Green Mountain State, and when you travel through it, a beautiful view seems to jump out around every corner.

Mountains and Valleys

Vermont sits in the northeastern corner of the United States, in the region known as New England. (The other New England states are Connecticut, Maine, Massachusetts, New Hampshire, and Rhode Island.) It is the only New England state with no coastline on the Atlantic Ocean. From north to south, Vermont is about 160 miles (260 kilometers) long,

Quick Facts

VERMONT BORDERS

North	Canada
South	Massachusetts
East	New Hampshire
West	New York

Vermont's Green Mountain National Forest covers nearly two-thirds of the length of the state.

and from east to west, it is 80 miles (130 km) wide on average, with a total land area of some 9,250 square miles (23,950 square kilometers). Only seven states are smaller in land area. But it is said that if Vermont's wrinkled mountains and valleys could be ironed out flat, the state would spread to the size of Texas. That would make Vermont almost thirty times bigger in land area.

The Green Mountains, Vermont's largest mountain range, run like a backbone down the center of the state. The slopes are covered with thick blankets of trees. The highest peak,

Quick Facts

VERMONT COUNTIES

Vermont has fourteen counties. Chittenden County has the biggest population by far (more than 150,000 people, or one out of every four people in the state). The state's biggest city, Burlington, is located in Chittenden County. The city sits on the shores of Lake Champlain.

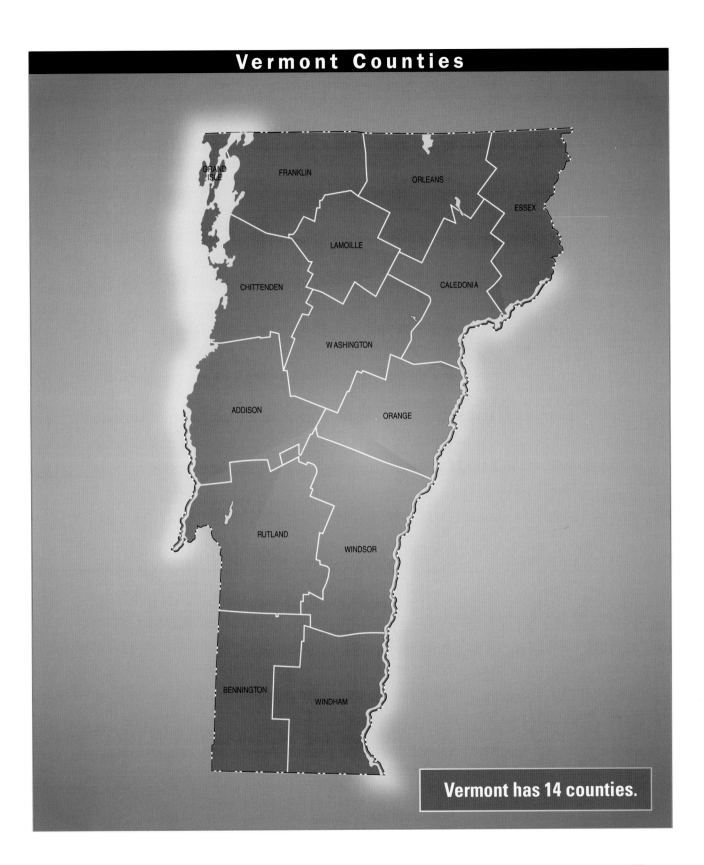

Vermont has 14 counties.

The peak of Owl's Head Mountain, in Groton State Forest, offers beautiful views.

Mount Mansfield, juts up 4,393 feet (1,339 meters) into the sky, making it the highest point in the state. Like other Vermont mountains, the Green Mountains were once much taller. The stone that makes up the Green Mountains has been worn down over millions of years. During the last Ice Age, which ended more than ten thousand years ago, thick sheets of slow-moving ice called glaciers scraped across the mountains. As the glaciers moved, they changed the shape of the land and transported huge amounts of sand, soil, and rock. Vermont still has huge rocks that the glaciers carried and left behind.

Many peaks in the Green Mountains are big enough to have names. A hiking path called the Long Trail runs from one peak to another. It stretches more than 270 miles (435 km), from the top of Vermont to the Massachusetts border. Forests, waterfalls, and dazzling views mark the way.

Quick Facts

A GIANT ROCK

One of the biggest rocks moved by a glacier is the so-called Green Mountain Giant. Located on a woodland trail in the southern part of the state, it is about 25 feet (8 m) high, 40 feet (12 m) long, and 125 feet (38 m) around. It is estimated to weigh some 6.8 million pounds (3 million kilograms).

To the east of the Green Mountains lies the Connecticut River valley, an area of quiet towns, woods, and green rolling hills. The Connecticut River forms the border between Vermont and New Hampshire. It flows gently south toward the bottom of New England. Smaller rivers, such as the White and West rivers, spill down the Green Mountains into the Connecticut River, rushing and swirling when the snow melts in spring.

Another valley spreads to the west of the Green Mountains. Lake Champlain is located in this valley. The lake stretches about half the length of the state,

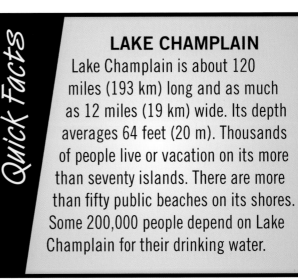

Chimney Point Bridge, which crosses Lake Champlain, connects Vermont and New York.

along the Vermont–New York border. It is fed in Vermont by the Missisquoi, Lamoille, and Winooski rivers and by Otter Creek, and it drains into the Richelieu River in the Canadian province of Quebec. From there the waters eventually reach the Atlantic Ocean. Along the eastern shores of the lake, dairy cows graze on some of Vermont's richest farmland. The state's biggest city, Burlington, sits on the lakeshore.

Climate

Vermont summers are usually mild, with warm days and cool nights. Morning mists often rise in the valleys, then dissolve into a clear blue sky. The average July temperature in Burlington is about 71 degrees Fahrenheit (22 degrees Celsius). Once in a while, a heat wave strikes. The hottest Vermont day on record was July 7, 1912, in Vernon, where the thermometer hit 107 °F (42 °C).

Autumn and winter can bring crisp, clear days, as well as wet weather. By January, the state is usually covered with a thick blanket of snow. Temperatures

When the snow falls, snowmobiling is a popular outdoor activity in Vermont.

drop below freezing, and icy winds chill the air even more. Vermont winters can be long and frigid. The average January temperature in Burlington is 18 °F (–8 °C). The coldest recorded day was December 30, 1933, in Bloomfield, where the temperature plunged to –50 °F (–46 °C).

Every year, Burlington receives about 40 inches (100 centimeters) of precipitation—melted snow, rain, and other moisture. The mountainous areas in the state get the most snow—an average of around 80 to 120 inches (200 to 300 cm) each year. The Connecticut River and Champlain Lake valleys receive less, averaging about 70 inches (180 cm) per year.

Around March, the ice and snow begin melting. But it takes weeks for spring to really arrive. Snow turns to slush, and tires sink into the muck on mountain roads. Vermonters call this period mud season. It is the one time of year many Vermonters prefer to stay inside.

Forests and Fields

Large areas of Vermont's forests were once cleared for farming, and by the late 1800s, only 20 to 30 percent of the land was forested. Although the woods have grown back, the remains of stone walls from old farms can often still be seen among the trees.

Outside the Champlain Lake valley, the state today is carpeted with woods, broken up by ribbons of roads and patches of farm fields and villages. In all, more than three-quarters of the land is wooded. The forests have more than one hundred kinds of trees. Evergreens include spruce, fir, hemlock, and cedar trees. Beside them grow deciduous trees, which lose their leaves in

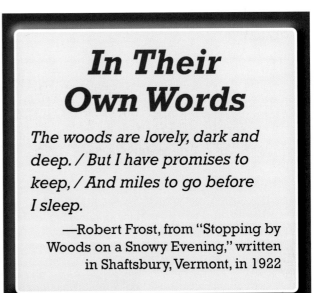

In Their Own Words

The woods are lovely, dark and deep. / But I have promises to keep, / And miles to go before I sleep.

—Robert Frost, from "Stopping by Woods on a Snowy Evening," written in Shaftsbury, Vermont, in 1922

Vermont's tree-covered countryside is a colorful sight in autumn.

the fall. These include maples and birches, along with ash, elm, beech, hickory, and poplar trees.

When autumn comes, it sets the woods glowing with brilliant colors. Beeches, ashes, and hickories turn different shades of yellow. Sugar maples turn amber, gold, and scarlet. Vermont's fall leaves are so bright that tourists come from other states and even foreign countries to catch the display. The amount of color varies from year to year, depending on weather conditions. Sunny fall days with cool nights help the leaves turn brightest. Fall color reports in newspapers and on the Internet—a little like weather reports—help "leaf peepers" (people on the lookout for bright fall colors) hit the best spots at the right times.

In winter months, the maples and other deciduous trees are bare and trimmed with snow. But just before the first buds of spring appear, the sap of sugar maples starts flowing. Vermonters tap them around this time and boil down the sweet liquid to produce maple syrup.

In spring and summer, delicate wildflowers bloom in the Vermont woods. White, yellow, and purple violets cluster between the roots of trees. Irises grow on the banks of streams, and bog laurel crowds mountain marshes. In September, goldenrods and purple asters fill Vermont meadows.

VERMONT'S STATE FLOWER

The red clover, which is often seen along Vermont's country roads, was named the state flower in 1894. Early European settlers brought this plant to the region. Farmers grow red clover to help fertilize their fields and to provide feed for cows and other farm animals.

Vermont has some flowering plants that are quite rare. One plant, Jesup's milk-vetch, grows in only a few places in the United States. A member of the pea family, it has bluish-purple flowers. It clings to the thin soil on rocks along the Connecticut River near Hartland. Jesup's milk-vetch is an endangered plant, that is, one in danger of becoming extinct, or completely dying out. People are not allowed to pick it, even if they own the land it grows on. State planners must also think carefully before threatening its habitat with major changes, such as constructing a dam that would make the river level rise.

Running Wild

The Vermont woods are rich in wildlife. Chipmunks dart between rocks, around trees, and over logs. These and many other forest animals lie low during much of the day and are most active around late afternoon or evening. White-tailed deer may nibble green twigs at sunset, and moose wade through rivers in the northeast woods. Beavers swim out from their lodges to chew on aspen trees. Rabbits leave their burrows to look for food. So do predators such as bobcats, minks, and foxes. Bears are also most active around twilight.

The cool lakes and rivers of the Green Mountain State are filled with fish. Big fish, such as landlocked salmon and northern pike, and small ones, such as smelt, share the deep waters of Lake Champlain. Perch, trout, and bass are among the many kinds of fish that live in rivers and streams. Many birds that live near the water, such as herons, egrets, kingfishers, and osprey, depend on the fish for food.

Two hundred years ago, the North American cougar—also called the puma, mountain lion, catamount, or panther—roamed the Green Mountains. This big cat, with its wild grace, once stood for the freedom of the Vermont frontier. But farmers and loggers cleared acres of forests, destroying the cougar's natural habitat. Hunters and trappers killed animals the big cats needed for food, as well as the cats themselves. Vermont's last known cougar was killed in 1881.

In fact, cougars have died out in most of the eastern United States. They are now listed by the federal government as an endangered species. In recent decades, hundreds of people have reported seeing cougars in Vermont, but so far there has been no confirmation that cougars are back. If the big cats ever did make a comeback, the remote woods in the northern part of the state would be a likely place for them.

The beaver is Vermont's largest rodent.

BLACK BEARS

Black bears are the smallest of the three bear species in North America. They are the only bears in Vermont. Though smaller than other types of bears, black bears are still large. An adult male usually weighs around 300 to 400 pounds (140 to 180 kg). Vermont is believed to be home to more than three thousand black bears. They like to stay hidden in the woods but may show up to look for food around campsites and garbage cans.

Cleaning Up

Vermont is a leading state when it comes to protecting the environment. But one challenge it still faces is keeping water life healthy. Lakes and ponds are especially threatened by phosphorus, a chemical that gets washed from farms, cities, and sewage treatment plants into the state's waterways. As

Protecting Vermont's ponds, lakes, and rivers is important to the state's many fishers.

To ensure clean water, scientists in Vermont regularly test samples from local lakes and rivers.

phosphorus builds up in lakes, it causes too much algae to grow. As the algae rapidly spreads, it can rob other plants and animals of needed oxygen until they sicken and die. One spot where algae have become a serious problem is Missisquoi Bay, in northern Lake Champlain.

Vermont citizens have helped the state monitor algae and phosphorus levels at different spots in Lake Champlain. This research gives scientists a rough idea of how much phosphorus is too much. In 2003, the state government announced its initial plans to deal with these and other environmental problems affecting Lake Champlain, and in 2010, the state of Vermont, along with New York state and the Canadian province of Quebec, agreed to a joint long-term management plan for the lake. It was aimed in part at reducing phosphorus levels, preventing contamination by toxic substances, and managing species that threaten the lake's ecosystem.

Plants & Animals

Red Maple

The red maple, also called the swamp maple, is one of the jewels of the Vermont woods. The state has a heavy concentration of these trees. They show red buds in winter, red flowers in spring, and red leaf stems in summer. But the red maple truly stands out in early fall. Its leaves turn a fiery red, even while most other trees remain green.

Little Brown Bat

The most common of the state's nine bat species, these mammals live in barns and attics in warm weather and in caves and old mines during the winter. They can eat half their body weight in insects each night. Like other bats, they find their way by "echolocation"—sending out sound waves that bounce back from objects. The bats have been dying in record numbers from a mysterious disease known as white-nose syndrome. Scientists are working on ways to stop the white fungus that grows on the muzzles and wings of bats and seems to cause their deaths.

Snowshoe Hare

On winter mornings, the Vermont woods are often crisscrossed with the tracks of snowshoe hares. These animals change color with the seasons. In early fall, they gradually replace their brown coat with white fur to match the winter snow. Snowshoe hares are also speedy. They may run as fast as 28 miles (45 km) an hour to escape a fox or an owl.

Wild Turkey

In the 1800s, Vermonters cleared so much land that many woodland animals, including the wild turkey, died out. But about forty years ago, biologists brought some wild turkeys back to Vermont. Their population increased rapidly, and wild turkeys now nest again in the Green Mountains, where they feed on nuts and berries. They are very alert and have excellent vision. These and other advantages help them survive in spite of their many predators.

Spring Peeper

The tiny frogs called spring peepers are easier to hear than they are to see. They perch on the grasses that grow near ponds and wetlands and loudly peep to find mates in spring. An adult spring peeper may measure less than 1 inch (2.5 cm), but it can jump as far as 1.5 feet (45 cm) to get away from enemies.

Chickadee

Black-capped chickadees live in Vermont all through the year. They often form small flocks and hop between branches of evergreen trees. When threatened by an intruder, a chickadee warns other birds with its familiar call of "chick-a-dee-dee-dee."

From the Beginning

More than ten thousand years ago, when the glaciers melted at the end of the last Ice Age, people called Paleo-Indians began moving into the land that is now Vermont. At the time, there were wide stretches of mostly open land. This land looked like the tundra in today's Arctic regions of the world. The weight of the glaciers had lowered the level of some of the land, creating a huge valley. Water from the ocean flowed into this valley and formed a big sea.

The Paleo-Indians probably camped in small groups along the shores of this saltwater sea. They may have caught fish, seals, and shellfish to eat. They may also have hunted the caribou that once roamed the land in gigantic herds. No one knows exactly what life was like for these early people. The only clues that have been found are spear tips and other stone tools.

Over the centuries, the climate got warmer, and the landscape slowly changed. The land crushed down by glaciers gradually rose back up. The saltwater sea dried up, and eventually a smaller freshwater lake, now known as Lake Champlain, was formed. Forests spread across the hills.

In time, the people learned to make pottery from clay. They still hunted and fished, and they also gathered food, such as acorns, hickory nuts, and raspberries, from the forest. Eventually, they learned to grow crops such as beans, squash, and corn.

The Bennington Battle Monument includes a statue of Seth Warner, a military leader who helped defeat the British in the Battle of Bennington during the American Revolution.

At the time European explorers first arrived in the region, villages dotted the shores of Lake Champlain and the Connecticut River. The villages belonged to an American Indian group called the Abenaki. Iroquois Indians lived in large numbers to the west of the lake, in an area that is now part of New York state. They visited and at times lived in parts of what is now Vermont, and they became enemies of the Abenaki.

The Abenaki lived in wigwams, made of wooden frames that were covered with wide strips of bark from birch, basswood, or elm trees. They also used birch bark for canoes and baskets. The lives of the Abenaki changed with the seasons. In winter, they paddled upstream to the mountains to hunt moose and deer. When spring was on its way, they collected sap from sugar maple trees to make maple syrup. In summer and fall, they tended their fields and gathered wild plants to make medicine. They dried meat, fish, berries, and corn to eat when the weather turned cold.

Newcomers Arrive

In July 1609, a group of Indian warriors from the Quebec region paddled into the great lake the Abenaki called Bitawbagok. With them were Samuel de Champlain, the French explorer and founding father of Quebec, and two white companions.

The group came face-to-face with a number of Iroquois. (The Iroquois were longtime enemies of the northern Indians accompanying the French.) Champlain fired his gun, killing two Iroquois leaders. In the battle that followed, the Iroquois, armed only with bows and arrows, were easily defeated. Many fled in fear of the strange men with powerful weapons.

In Their Own Words

We entered the lake, which is of great extent, say eighty or a hundred leagues long, where I saw four fine islands. . . . There are also many rivers falling into the lake, bordered by many fine trees.

—Explorer Samuel de Champlain, in a 1609 journal entry describing the lake that is now named after him

Champlain named the lake after himself and claimed the land around it for France. As far as anyone knows, he and his men were the first Europeans to see the lake.

The Abenaki were not a part of this battle, and they never met Champlain. But they saw many changes soon after his arrival. More Frenchmen followed in Champlain's footsteps. They bought furs from the Abenaki in return for cotton cloth, iron pots, glass beads, and other goods new to the Abenaki. The French wanted a good relationship with the Abenaki and supplied them with guns and ammunition that could help them fight their enemies.

In 1666, a French captain named Pierre La Motte, sent by King Louis XIV, built a fort in the wilderness on an island in Lake Champlain (an island later

During the 1600s, French explorer Samuel de Champlain claimed Lake Champlain and the land around it for France. He is shown here battling Iroquois Indians near Lake Champlain.

Isle La Motte, on Lake Champlain, was the site of the first French, and first European, settlement in what is now Vermont. On the island is a statue honoring French explorer Samuel de Champlain.

named after La Motte). The fort, named Saint Anne, protected French territory from attack. Fort Saint Anne was the first European settlement in what is now Vermont. Other French forts and villages sprang up along the lakeshore. On the other side of the Green Mountains, in 1724, British soldiers of the Massachusetts militia built Fort Dummer as a frontier defense against French and Indian forces. This fort, on the Connecticut River, opened up permanent settlement by British colonists in what is now southeastern Vermont.

As Europeans pushed in from both sides, clashes broke out. Indians, except for the Iroquois, mostly sided with the French. In the French and Indian War, which began in 1754, the Abenaki helped capture more than a thousand British settlers. They marched their prisoners north through present-day Vermont to lands controlled by France. Some prisoners died on the way, but many lived to tell their stories. They painted a vivid picture of the Indians and the wild country they had traveled through.

The Abenaki people, however, were under pressure from expanding British settlements. Most of them moved north toward present-day Canada, leaving lands their ancestors had occupied for centuries. The French suffered key defeats in the region, including the loss of Fort Ticonderoga in New York, on the western shore of Lake Champlain. In 1763, the French signed a peace treaty, ending the war.

The Green Mountain Boys

With the treaty of 1763, the British won control of virtually all of eastern North America. Even before then, British settlers were clearing new land. The royal governor of New Hampshire, Benning Wentworth, sold many pieces of land—known as grants—in the area just to the west of the Green Mountains. By 1770, hundreds of people from Massachusetts and Connecticut owned, or believed they owned, these lands.

Wentworth claimed that this land was owned by the New Hampshire colony. However, in the eyes of the British government, it belonged to the colony of New York. New York officials tried to make the land-grant settlers leave or pay rent on their farms. Most of them refused, and they teamed up to defend their property.

Their leader, a settler named Ethan Allen, went to a court in Albany, New York, to plead their case. But the court rejected his argument. According to one account, he reacted with a remark that is now famous among Vermonters: "The gods of the hills are not the gods of the valley." In other words, he believed that New Yorkers would lose out in the end.

After the court decision, in 1770, Allen gathered about two hundred men to fight for the New Hampshire grants. They called themselves the Green Mountain Boys. Instead of wearing uniforms, they wore evergreen twigs in their caps. They harassed and sought to drive away settlers who sided with New York.

A New Republic

At first, New Yorkers called the Green Mountain Boys "rioters and traitors." But when the colonies began fighting for independence from Great Britain, this militia was an important part of the patriot cause. In May 1775, soon after the first shots of the American Revolution had been fired, the Green Mountain Boys, led by Ethan Allen and Seth Warner, captured Fort Ticonderoga from the British. When New York leaders found out, they actually paid the men and bought them uniforms.

Most settlers in the New Hampshire grants believed in the American Revolution. But they did not want their territory to be part of New York. So in January 1777, at a meeting in the town of Westminster, leaders in the region proclaimed it to be "a separate and independent state, or government." It was later named the Republic of Vermont, based on the French words *vert mont*, which mean "green mountain."

In July 1777, Vermont leaders gathered at a tavern in the town of Windsor to adopt a constitution for their independent republic. It was the first such constitution to outlaw slavery. It was also the first to give all men twenty-one

Leaders met in this Windsor building to sign Vermont's historic constitution in 1777.

Every year on August 16, Vermonters in Bennington reenact the famous battle fought nearby, on that day in 1777.

years old or older the right to vote, whether or not they owned land. In addition, the Vermont constitution was the first to authorize a system of public schools.

In 1778, Vermonters elected a group of representatives called the Vermont Assembly. Vermonters wanted their "republic" to be represented in the Continental Congress formed by the American colonies now fighting for their independence. However, because of New York's opposition, this did not happen.

Earlier, the Vermonters built a fort on the eastern side of Lake Champlain, opposite Fort Ticonderoga. They were forced to abandon it when a British force of seven thousand men moved into the area from Canada. But in August 1777, the Green Mountain Boys, now led by Seth Warner, joined forces with patriot troops, and together they defeated the British in the so-called Battle of Bennington. (It was actually fought in what is now New York state, near Bennington.) A few months later, the British were defeated at Saratoga, New York. This

Quick Facts

THE ROYALTON RAID
On October 16, 1780, a British regiment, joined by some three hundred Iroquois, raided the town of Royalton and many homesteads along Vermont's White River. They burned houses and barns and slaughtered livestock. They killed four Americans and captured twenty-seven others, who were taken back to Canada.

was the last battle fought in or near Vermont during the American Revolution, but the British and their Indian allies raided towns in Vermont throughout the war.

The Fourteenth State

The American Revolution ended with a treaty signed in Paris in 1783. Under this treaty, the British finally recognized American independence. With the country at peace, Vermont's population climbed. By 1785, Vermont had its own newspaper and post offices. The tiny republic even issued its own copper coins.

In 1790, New York and Vermont finally came to an agreement. Vermont promised to pay New York $30,000 to put old arguments to rest. In 1791, the Vermont Assembly voted 105 to 2 to adopt the U.S. Constitution. That same year, every member of the U.S. Congress voted to accept Vermont as the fourteenth state. Thomas Chittenden, who had been governor of the Vermont republic, was elected as the first governor of the new state.

Vermont had about 85,000 people when it joined the Union—almost three times as many as when the republic was formed. Over the next twenty years, it became the nation's fastest-growing state. New settlers cleared land for farming. They built sawmills along streams and dug canals to help boats carry goods between towns.

The settlers did not have an easy life. Farming the rocky soil of the Green Mountains was backbreaking work. Some years, heavy rainstorms made streams overflow and wash away bridges and barns. Other years saw almost no rain at all.

Quick Facts

PEOPLE AND SHEEP
Vermonters started raising a lot of sheep during the War of 1812, when the country needed wool. By 1840, Vermont had six times as many sheep as people. In the 1850s, however, when sheep farming spread to the wide open spaces farther west, the industry in Vermont declined.

Building a Future

Many Vermonters opposed the War of 1812, a conflict between the United States and Great Britain. They did not want it to disrupt the state's trade with Canada, which was then still a British possession. However, patriotic volunteers from Vermont went to New York to help defend the town of Plattsburg in September 1814, near the end of the war.

Times were difficult after the war ended in 1815. Cheap goods from Britain became available, forcing many Vermonters out of business. Manufacturing jobs were in short supply. A long-lasting frost in 1816 destroyed crops. Many farmers moved farther west, where land was better and more plentiful.

As the nation grappled with the issue of slavery in the mid–1800s, Vermonters became involved. They had already outlawed slavery in their state. They now promoted efforts to move free blacks back to Africa. They also sheltered escaped slaves from the South who were traveling north to Canada along a secret route called the Underground Railroad. The "railroad" was a network of homes, churches, and other places where escaped slaves could rest and receive food and other needed supplies as they journeyed north. Vermont also passed legislation to keep slave owners from capturing escaped slaves in the state and taking them back.

In 1861, the Civil War broke out between the North and South. Vermont was the first state to offer troops to the North. About 35,000 Vermont men fought in the war, and some 10,000 were killed or disabled.

This painting shows a Vermont regiment in action during the Civil War. Some 35,000 Vermonters fought for the North in that war.

After the war ended in 1865 with a Northern victory, slavery was abolished nationwide.

In the years following the Civil War, agriculture continued to decline in Vermont. Many people left to try their luck in other parts of the country. Some Vermonters who stayed on earned their living raising dairy cows. The state's dairy farms became famous for their milk, cheese, and butter. Other people found work in Burlington lumber mills. Still others worked in factories making machine tools. And once railroads had been built to help transport heavy goods, Vermont became a leading source for granite and marble used nationwide.

Some Vermont businesses brought in workers from other parts of the world. Scottish, Spanish, and Italian immigrants cut and carved granite in Barre. People from Poland, Spain, Greece, and Russia worked for the Vermont Marble Company in Proctor.

New Vermont

In both World War I (1914–1918) and World War II (1939–1945), Vermont's industries supplied clothing, machine tools, lumber, and other goods to help the war efforts. Some 16,000 Vermonters served in the armed forces in World War I, which the United States entered in 1917, and about 40,000 served in World War II, which the United States entered in 1941.

Between these wars, in 1927, a severe flood destroyed roads, bridges, and homes in Vermont, killing 85 people and leaving 9,000 homeless. In the Great Depression of the 1930s, a time of severe economic hardship nationwide, some 50,000 Vermonters lost their jobs. The Civilian Conservation Corps, created by

Located in the Connecticut River valley, Brattleboro was a bustling city and center of commerce in the early 1900s.

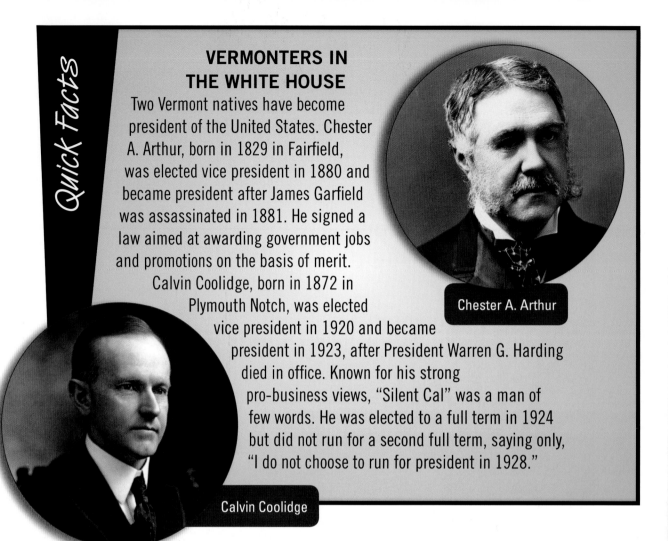

VERMONTERS IN THE WHITE HOUSE

Two Vermont natives have become president of the United States. Chester A. Arthur, born in 1829 in Fairfield, was elected vice president in 1880 and became president after James Garfield was assassinated in 1881. He signed a law aimed at awarding government jobs and promotions on the basis of merit.

Calvin Coolidge, born in 1872 in Plymouth Notch, was elected vice president in 1920 and became president in 1923, after President Warren G. Harding died in office. Known for his strong pro-business views, "Silent Cal" was a man of few words. He was elected to a full term in 1924 but did not run for a second full term, saying only, "I do not choose to run for president in 1928."

Chester A. Arthur

Calvin Coolidge

President Franklin D. Roosevelt, put many back to work. Workers built state parks, highways, and other facilities, including a number of dams intended to prevent a repeat of the 1927 flood disaster.

During the late 1800s, the state had begun to attract summer visitors, who were eager for the chance to hunt, fish, or experience country life on a farm. But it was not until the 1930s that Vermonters learned to make the most of their steep slopes and winter snowstorms. When Americans took up skiing, Vermonters realized they had "white gold." The first ski lift in the United States was built in Woodstock in 1934. The simple towrope that took skiers to the top of the slope got its power from the engine of a Ford Model T automobile. Six years later, the nation's first chairlift started carrying skiers in Stowe.

Vermont became known as a vacation spot thanks to the ski season. Many skiers came back in summer and fell in love with the quiet, unspoiled land. And a major road-building program in the late 1950s helped open up the state to greater numbers of visitors.

By the 1960s, people who wanted to escape from the cities found Vermont a great place to start new lives. Some young men and women who wanted to get

The city of Montpelier was hard-hit by the flood of 1927, one of the most disastrous floods in Vermont's history.

Vermont continues to attract vacationers and residents alike. Here visitors to downtown Burlington stroll along Church Street.

closer to nature began small farms in Vermont. Vacation houses popped up in the mountains and around lakes. Many writers and artists also relocated. Today, Vermont has about two-thirds more people than it did in the 1950s. The state has more buildings, more traffic, and more roads as well. But it also has more laws and programs to protect Vermont's environment and rural character.

In 1968, a grassroots effort spurred lawmakers to pass a measure banning all billboards on Vermont highways. In 1970, legislators passed the Environmental Control Law, also known as Act 250, which allows the state to limit development based on its impact on the environment. Also in 1970, the state government launched Vermont's first Green-Up Day. The event, now organized by a private nonprofit company, is held every year on the first Saturday in May. Vermont children take the day to clean up litter in parks and along roadways and waterways throughout the state. These and other steps have helped preserve the state's natural beauty.

Important Dates

★ **c. 8000** BCE Early peoples begin moving into what is now Vermont.

★ **1609** Samuel de Champlain enters Lake Champlain and claims the land around it for France.

★ **1666** French soldiers build a fort on Isle La Motte, creating Vermont's first European settlement.

★ **1724** British troops build the first permanent European settlement, called Fort Dummer.

★ **1749** Governor Benning Wentworth makes the first New Hampshire grant, for the town of Bennington.

★ **1770** Ethan Allen organizes a force of two hundred men called the Green Mountain Boys to protect the New Hampshire grants from New York.

★ **1777** Vermont declares itself an independent republic.

★ **1791** Vermont becomes the fourteenth U.S. state.

★ **1805** Montpelier is chosen as Vermont's capital city.

★ **1864** Confederate soldiers raid St. Albans during the Civil War.

★ **1881** Chester A. Arthur becomes the country's twenty-first president.

★ **1923** Calvin Coolidge becomes the thirtieth U.S. president.

★ **1934** The first ski lift in the United States is built in Woodstock.

★ **1968** Vermont lawmakers ban billboards on roadways.

★ **1970** Lawmakers pass Act 250, allowing the state to regulate land use based on impact on the environment.

★ **1984** Vermont elects its first woman governor, Madeleine M. Kunin.

★ **2003** Former governor Howard Dean begins his candidacy for U.S. president.

★ **2009** Vermont lawmakers vote to allow same-sex marriages in the state.

★ **2011** Heavy rains from Hurricane Irene cause widespread flooding. Many homes, farms, businesses, roads, and bridges are damaged or destroyed. About a dozen communities are temporarily isolated, without power or freshwater.

The People

More than 625,000 people live in Vermont today. But that is a small number compared to most other states. Wyoming is the only state with fewer people. Vermont is mostly forests, farms, and villages, not big cities. Its heart is in the country, and Vermonters tend to be proud of their ties with the land. They are also known for valuing freedom and independence. Dorothy Canfield Fisher, a well-known Vermont writer and educational reformer, once said there was an unwritten law that every Vermonter "must be allowed to do, think, believe whatever seems best to him."

Vermonters Old and New

About half the people who live in Vermont were born in the state. Many have Vermont roots that go back many generations. Dairy farmer Rosina Wallace still works in the fields bought by her great-grandparents in the 1800s. "Farming is tiring and hard work, but I grew up on this farm," says Wallace.

Quick Facts

CITIES OF THE GREEN MOUNTAIN STATE

Burlington, the largest city in Vermont, has about 42,000 residents. Essex, with almost 20,000; South Burlington, with almost 18,000; Colchester with 17,000; and Rutland, with about 16,000, are the next-largest cities and towns. Montpelier, Vermont's capital city since 1805, has fewer than 8,000 residents. It is by far the smallest capital city in the nation.

At farms across Vermont, families select pumpkins to decorate for Halloween.

Newcomers are attracted to Vermont's many opportunities. This Vermonter works raising organic produce.

"I love the view almost as much as scratching a cow behind the ears." Other Vermont families have a long tradition of working in granite quarries or lumber mills.

But Vermont has also attracted newcomers from other states. Some were vacationers who decided to stay year-round, perhaps to raise children or enjoy retirement in a comfortable environment. A few started organic farms, raising animals and growing crops without chemical fertilizers or pesticides. Others built businesses selling traditional crafts such as handmade furniture or pottery. Many others found jobs in education, health care, or manufacturing.

People who migrated from other states have become as much a part of Vermont as those whose families lived there for generations. Jay Craven is a filmmaker who moved from New York to Vermont in 1974. He makes movies right near his home in St. Johnsbury and enjoys working with small-town communities. "Vermont has a traditional conservatism," says Craven, "which basically says that for things to change they should change only for good reason. But once the good reason is presented, things do change. There is an openness in Vermont by people to respect all points of view."

The population has remained mostly Caucasian, or white. In fact, according to the 2010 Census, Vermont still has a larger proportion of white residents than any other state. Asians and African Americans each make up only about 1 percent of the state's population. Hispanic Americans, who may be of any race, represent about 1.5 percent. Before European settlement, the region's entire population was American Indian. Today, however, American Indians represent only a tiny minority in the state.

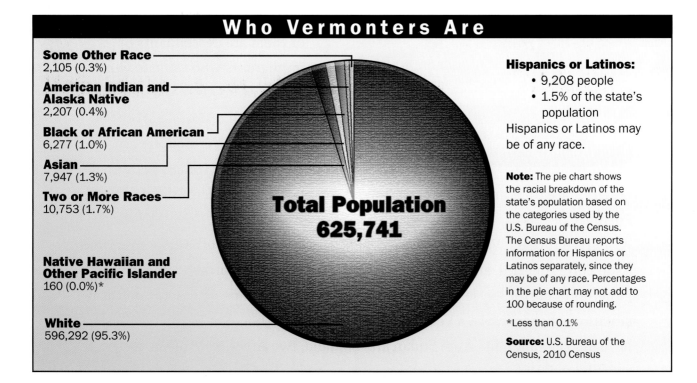

Who Vermonters Are

Some Other Race
2,105 (0.3%)

American Indian and Alaska Native
2,207 (0.4%)

Black or African American
6,277 (1.0%)

Asian
7,947 (1.3%)

Two or More Races
10,753 (1.7%)

Native Hawaiian and Other Pacific Islander
160 (0.0%)*

White
596,292 (95.3%)

Total Population 625,741

Hispanics or Latinos:
• 9,208 people
• 1.5% of the state's population
Hispanics or Latinos may be of any race.

Note: The pie chart shows the racial breakdown of the state's population based on the categories used by the U.S. Bureau of the Census. The Census Bureau reports information for Hispanics or Latinos separately, since they may be of any race. Percentages in the pie chart may not add to 100 because of rounding.

*Less than 0.1%

Source: U.S. Bureau of the Census, 2010 Census

An Asian-American family has fun sledding in Vermont's Bolton Valley.

Many Vermonters are typical Yankees, tracing their ancestry to the British Isles. These people account for more than one-fourth of the population today. But a good number of French Canadians moved from the province of Quebec into mill towns and farms over the border in Vermont during the early 1900s. People of French or French-Canadian descent account for another one-fourth of the current population.

Among other nationalities, around one-fifth of today's Vermonters are Irish. Many of them are descendants of immigrants who came to work on the railroads in the mid-nineteenth century. Large numbers of Vermonters are of German or Italian descent. Others trace their ancestry back to Poland, Scandinavia, the Netherlands, Portugal, or Russia.

In recent years, Vermont has welcomed a greater number of immigrants from Asia, Latin America, and Africa. While these immigrants typically came in search of better opportunity, some were refugees seeking to escape dangerous political situations. For example, a Vermont refugee program that started in 2001 has brought in immigrants from Sudan and Somalia, two African countries torn apart by civil war.

In recent years, Vermont has welcomed growing numbers of immigrants from all parts of the world. This refugee from Sudan works as a wood carver in Burlington.

Beginning life over in a new part of the world is often lonely and difficult, but it can also bring hope. Ibrahim Jafar, from Somalia, brought his family to Winooski in 2003. "We knew only that we were going to a strange land, to a place we never heard of, a city we never heard of," he said during a welcome ceremony at Winooski's city hall. "Already it seems like home."

Famous Vermonters

Ethan Allen: Green Mountain Rebel

Born in Connecticut in 1738, Ethan Allen settled in what is now Vermont and organized a militia called the Green Mountain Boys to fight against efforts by New Yorkers to take control of the territory. During the American Revolution, Allen led his men in battle against the British, taking Fort Ticonderoga in 1775. He was captured by the British during an ill-fated campaign against Canada, and he described his time in prison in a popular book called *A Narrative of Colonel Ethan Allen's Captivity*. He died in 1789.

George Dewey: Military Leader

Born in 1837 in Montpelier, George Dewey entered the U.S. Navy and took part in the 1862 capture of New Orleans, Louisiana, during the Civil War. At the outbreak of the Spanish–American War in 1898, Dewey, who commanded the U.S. naval squadron in the Pacific, destroyed the Spanish fleet in Manila Bay, the Philippines, without losing a single American life. Promoted soon after to the special rank of Admiral of the Navy, he was one of the most popular American military figures of this era. He died in 1917.

Robert Frost: Poet

Born in California in 1874, Robert Frost spent most of his life in New England, where he wrote poetry, taught in colleges, and farmed. While living in the Vermont countryside in the 1920s, he wrote some of his best-known poems, including "Stopping by Woods on a Snowy Evening." Frost earned four Pulitzer Prizes for his poetry. He died in 1963 and is buried in Bennington.

Norman Rockwell: Illustrator

Norman Rockwell was born in New York City in 1894. He lived and worked in Arlington, Vermont, from 1939 to 1953. In his pictures, especially for the covers of the *Saturday Evening Post* and other popular magazines, he depicted scenes from small-town life in loving detail. Some popular works include a family having Thanksgiving dinner, children sledding, and girls getting drinks at a soda fountain. Rockwell received the Presidential Medal of Freedom in 1978. He died the following year.

Jody Williams: Human Rights Activist

Born in Brattleboro in 1950, Jody Williams graduated from the University of Vermont and went on to become a world leader in the fight against the use of land mines. These explosives, often left in place after a war has ended, can kill or cripple anyone who sets them off. To end their use and aid land mine survivors, Williams helped form a group called the International Campaign to Ban Landmines (ICBL). In 1997, Williams and the ICBL were awarded the Nobel Peace Prize.

Patty Sheehan: Golfer

Born in Middlebury in 1956, Patty Sheehan was a downhill skier in her childhood. She started concentrating on golf when she was eighteen. She ended up winning five major women's golf championships during the 1980s and 1990s, and in 1993, she was inducted into the World Golf Hall of Fame. Later, she began playing on the senior golf circuit.

Celebrating the Arts

The arts are a big part of life in Vermont. Some of the state's most popular art forms go back to when the state first formed. Others are new and experimental. In a number of Vermont towns, dancers still swing their partners to old-time New England fiddle tunes. People of all ages enjoy what is known as contra dancing. This is a local tradition similar to square dancing except that the couples face each other in rows.

Vermont is an important center for crafts such as woodworking, weaving, pottery, and glassblowing. Many of the artists involved are inspired by past traditions. Jeanne Brink makes baskets the way her Abenaki grandmother did long ago, weaving them out of thin strips of wood and grasses. She learned from an older basket maker, who asked her to promise to keep the craft within the Abenaki people. "I will only teach Abenaki how to make ash-splint and sweet grass baskets," says Brink, "to keep it an Abenaki tradition."

People have been making quilts in Vermont since before the American Revolution. A quilter might stitch hundreds of different pieces of cloth together to form a pattern or picture. Quilts that are two hundred years old or more can be found in the Shelburne Museum near Burlington. Historian Richard Cleveland sees them as pieces of the state's past. "Sometimes when I find a quilt I especially like," he says, "I run the tips of my fingers gently over its surface, willing it to tell me its secrets."

Quilters from around the state and around the country come to Northfield every June or July for the Vermont Quilt Festival. It is said to be New England's oldest and largest annual quilt event.

One Vermont group, the Bread and Puppet Theater, took a very old art form and made it into something new. This group was founded in New York City in the 1960s but subsequently relocated to Vermont. Theater members use music, dance, and puppets of all sizes—including figures that tower some 8 feet (2.5 m) high—to entertain, but also to promote the group's own political messages. The Bread and Puppet Theater, which travels during much of the year, presents free outdoor shows in summer on a farm near Glover.

ARTS AND EDUCATION

Vermont has about twenty colleges and universities. One of the best-known is the University of Vermont, in Burlington. It is one of the oldest colleges in the United States, dating back to 1791. Now a relatively small, high-ranked public university, it has about 14,000 students.

Middlebury College, in the Green Mountains, is a well-respected private liberal arts college with about 2,300 undergraduate students. Many people attend its well-known English and foreign language programs, as well as its Bread Loaf Writers' Conference, which has brought together talented writers and interested students each summer since 1926.

The University of Vermont, in Burlington, attracts both Vermonters and students from out of state with its pleasant surroundings, relaxed atmosphere, and high academic standards.

MAKING A TIN-PUNCH LANTERN

Since the 1700s, Yankee tinsmiths have been creating useful household items such as trays, candleholders, cookie cutters, cookware, and teapots. They have also made punched-tin tiles to decorate ceilings, pie cupboards, and lanterns. Follow these instructions to make your own tin-punch lantern.

WHAT YOU NEED

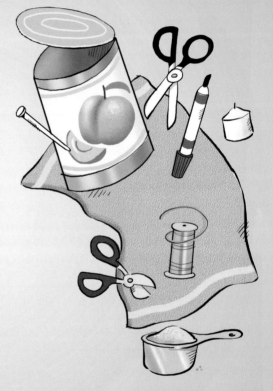

An empty can

Scissors

Water

Marker

Thick towel

Awl or large nail

Hammer

Copper wire, about 10 to 12 inches (25 to 30 cm) long

Wire cutters

Pliers

Votive candle (or battery-powered light used in jack-o'-lanterns on Halloween)

A few handfuls of sand

Pencil

Find an adult to assist you with this project. With your adult assistant, begin by preparing the empty can. Be careful of any sharp edges on the rim. Have your adult assistant file down the sharp edges. Then, wash out the can and remove the label—if there is one—with the scissors. Fill the can with water nearly to the top and put it in the freezer for several hours.

Once the water is frozen, use the marker to draw on the outside of the can. You can make shapes, a design that you like, or just a random pattern.

Find a sturdy work surface such as a table, workbench, or concrete floor. Fold a towel and place the can on it to keep it from slipping while you work. Have your adult assistant help you set the awl or large nail along your drawings.

Gently tap the awl or nail with the hammer. The awl or nail will punch through to the ice. You do not have to drive the nail in any deeper. Punch holes along the rest of your design. Make two larger holes near the top of the can, opposite from each other. These holes will be used for the handle.

Place the can in a sink or bucket and wait for the ice to start melting. When you are able, empty the can.

Measure and cut the copper wire with the wire cutters. Then, thread one end of the wire through one of the handle holes and wrap it around itself to make it secure. Use the pliers to squeeze the end of the wire so that no sharp ends are sticking out. Next, wrap the middle portion of the wire loosely around the pencil to make a spiral handle. Thread the wire through the other hole and wrap it around to secure the loop, using the pliers to squeeze the end.

Fill the bottom of the can with about 1 inch (2.5 cm) of sand. Place the candle inside. Have your adult assistant light the candle so that you can watch your lantern glow!

WARNING: Never light matches or candles without adult supervision. Make sure your lantern is far from papers, walls, or anything else that could catch fire. Be careful when handling the lantern because the metal can become very hot, and never leave your lit lantern unattended.

The Rugged Life

One thing nearly all Vermonters have in common is their love for the outdoors. In summer they may head for the Green Mountains to camp, hike, or take a dip in a sparkling lake or clear flowing stream. Almost two-thirds of Vermonters say they like to watch wildlife. That number is more than in any other state.

Fishing is a popular activity even during the winter months, when lakes and rivers are iced over. The temperature might be below zero, but the reward could be a hefty lake trout, walleye, or northern pike—or just good company. Winter, of course, is also time for skiing, snowboarding, and snowmobiling.

Despite Vermont's attractions, everyone who lives there has to face icy winters, muddy springs, and roller-coaster weather. That might be one reason people like to argue about what it takes to be a "real" Vermonter. Some say it means having great-grandparents who were born in the state. To others,

Kids in Vermont make the most of outdoor life, whether hiking in the hills, skiing on the slopes, or swimming in a mountain lake.

it means sticking with the place through thick and thin, even if you come from somewhere else.

The latter was the view of the late Graham Newell, a state senator from a seven-generation Vermont family. "I'm not one of those who says you've got to be born here to be a Vermonter," he once remarked. "If you are a Vermonter, you feel like one and you don't have to explain it."

During the winter, Vermonters fish in frozen lakes around the state, including Lake Shaftsbury in the Green Mountain National Forest.

Calendar of Events

★ Stowe Winter Carnival

At this January festival, kids can play snow volleyball, watch an ice-carving contest, or join a race through the woods on cross-country skis.

★ U.S. Open Snowboarding Championships in Stratton

Snowboarders become acrobats at this action-packed event in March. Visitors crowd around the half-pipe to watch daredevil twists and turns.

★ Vermont Maple Festival in St. Albans

Every spring, buckets of sap flow from sugar maple trees to make maple syrup. St. Albans celebrates the harvest in April with maple exhibits, a pancake breakfast, carnival rides, the 8.5-mile (14-km) "sap run" race, and a parade.

★ Plymouth Cheese and Harvest Festival in Plymouth Notch

This harvest celebration takes place in September at the site of President Calvin Coolidge's family home. Visitors can see what it's like to sheer a sheep or play games at home on a farm. They can also tour the cheese factory first opened by Coolidge's father.

★ Abenaki Heritage Celebration in Swanton

One day in late May, American Indians from Vermont and beyond come together on the village green to dance, make music, share traditional foods and crafts, and share Abenaki culture with others.

★ Vermont Dairy Festival in Enosburg Falls

There are lots of events during this dairy farm festival in June. Among other things, visitors can pet prize-winning cows, watch a milking contest, or tap their toes to live country music. Another highlight is the annual 6.2-mile (10-km) "milk run" race.

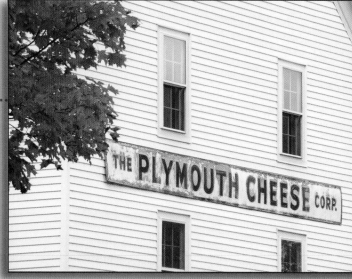

★ Vermont History Expo

In June, the Vermont Historical Society presents this event at the World's Fair Grounds in Tunbridge. Highlights include historical exhibits, a parade, performances, craft displays, auctions, and other fun activities.

★ Burlington Latino Festival

In September, Vermont's biggest city throws a multicultural fiesta that includes music, food, and dancing from Mexico, Cuba, Central America, and Puerto Rico.

★ Bondville Fair in Winhall

This fair is almost as old as the state of Vermont, and it has not changed much over the years. People come every August to eat fried dough, play horseshoes, and see how much weight a team of oxen can pull.

★ New World Festival in Randolph

Each September, Vermonters come to Randolph to celebrate their Celtic and French-Canadian roots with a fun-filled day of old-time music, dancing, and storytelling.

★ Vermont State Fair in Rutland

A September tradition for almost 170 years, the state fair in Rutland shows off farm animals and offers carnival rides along with plenty of food, games, prizes, and family fun.

★ Ethan Allen Days in Bennington

Music and food from Vermont's early days are among the highlights of this October celebration. Visitors travel back in time as history fans re-create battles from the American Revolution.

★ Vermont Apple Festival and Craft Show in Springfield

This October event offers a taste of country life in the Connecticut River valley, with folk music, hayrides, a craft contest, and (maybe best of all) plenty of crisp ripe apples.

4

How the Government Works

E ver since the time of the Green Mountain Boys, Vermonters have been ready to fight for what they believe in. They have also been willing to work together to shape Vermont's future. Citizens may come from different backgrounds, but when they speak out and share their ideas, they often find common ground.

Town and County

Close to home, Vermont gives citizens a great way to make their voices heard: the town meeting. There are 237 towns and nine cities in Vermont, and most of them hold such a meeting every year, usually on the first Tuesday in March. Anyone who is old enough to vote can join in.

At town meetings, citizens elect officials, approve budgets, and pass laws. They can also speak out if they disagree with a decision or want to suggest a new law. The town meeting is a New England tradition that goes back to the 1700s. It is often hailed as an outstanding example of democracy at work.

Quick Facts

MOTTO
Vermont's state motto is "Freedom and Unity." Ira Allen, Ethan Allen's brother and a fellow Green Mountain Boy, created this motto in 1777. Even today, the motto represents Vermonters' devotion to balancing the rights of individuals with the good of the community.

One role of county government in Vermont is to maintain a system of courts. This courthouse, in Windham County, is located in Newfane.

The state's fourteen counties are less important as units of government than are the cities and towns. However, counties do perform certain functions, especially maintaining a system of courts.

Federal and State Government

At the national level, Vermont, like every state big or small, elects two U.S. senators. But, as the second-smallest of the fifty states, Vermont elects only one member to the U.S. House of Representatives, where a state's number of seats is based on its population. Vermont's three federal lawmakers represent the interests of the state and its citizens in Washington, D.C. Senators serve six-year terms. Members of the House serve two years. There is no limit on the number of terms a member of Congress can serve.

The state government is responsible for matters that affect Vermont as a whole. The state has a major role to play in education, transportation, environmental protection, business and economic growth, public health, and public safety. Like the federal government and other state

Vermont's capitol, in Montpelier, is one of the oldest and best-preserved statehouses in the nation.

Branches of Government

EXECUTIVE ★ ★ ★ ★ ★ ★ ★ ★

The governor is the state's chief executive officer. He or she runs various departments of the state government and appoints top officials and judges. The governor also can approve or reject proposed laws. Unlike most other states, Vermont elects its governor to two-year terms. (Four-year terms are more common.) A governor can be reelected an unlimited number of times.

LEGISLATIVE ★ ★ ★ ★ ★ ★ ★ ★

Vermont's legislature, the general assembly, is made up of two bodies—the senate and the house of representatives. The senate has 30 members, each of whom represents one or more counties. The house has 150 members, representing about 4,000 citizens each. All lawmakers are elected to serve for two years, with no term limits. The legislature meets to hammer out new laws between January and late spring. Most of the members also have other jobs, such as running a business, practicing law, teaching school, or farming.

JUDICIAL ★ ★ ★ ★ ★ ★ ★ ★

Vermont's highest court is the supreme court, headed by a chief justice and also including four associate justices. They serve six-year terms and are appointed by the governor. The supreme court mainly hears appeals of cases decided in lower courts. These include superior courts, for civil cases such as lawsuits, and district courts, for criminal cases. Vermont also has family courts for divorce and child support cases, probate courts for wills, and an environmental court for land use disputes. The supreme court has the power to strike down a state law if it judges that the law violates the state constitution.

governments, Vermont's government is made up of three branches: executive, legislative, and judicial. Each branch has its own duties and responsibilities.

Most state offices are located in Montpelier, and the state legislature meets in the statehouse there. In addition to being the smallest state capital in the nation, Montpelier is one of the state's smaller cities. Most of its businesses fit on one main street. But its tiny size may be a good thing. It is an easy place for ordinary citizens to meet lawmakers face-to-face.

How a Bill Becomes a Law

The members of Vermont's legislature, or general assembly, make the state's laws. The first step is to put together a proposed law, or bill, and introduce it, or bring it before the state senate or house of representatives. Only a member of the legislature can introduce bills, but anyone can suggest a law to a legislator.

After a bill is introduced, it goes to a committee for discussion. Sometimes the committee holds a public hearing, where Vermonters can speak for or against the measure. The committee may reject the bill or support it, either as is or with changes. If and when the committee decides the bill is acceptable, it is read before the whole house or senate. That is when all members debate the bill and take a vote.

If a bill passes in one house of the general assembly, it then goes to the other, where all these steps have to be repeated. A bill often goes through many changes before the general assembly is done with it.

Vermont representatives debate budgetary issues in the house chamber of the Montpelier statehouse.

If all goes smoothly, the bill finally comes to the governor's desk. If the governor signs it, the bill becomes law. But the governor can also veto, or reject, a bill. Then it can become law only if two-thirds of both houses vote to "override" the veto. Each year, hundreds of bills are introduced to the general assembly. Out of that number, perhaps one in three eventually becomes a law.

Laws That Made It

Vermont may seem old-fashioned at times, but it has enacted some bold laws, especially related to protecting the environment. Vermont became the first state to outlaw billboards. In 1970, the general assembly passed Act 250, also called the Environmental Control Law, the first statewide land use law in the United States. This law says that before a new construction project can begin, it must ordinarily be approved by a committee of citizens appointed by the governor. This committee reviews the project's impact on the environment and plays a key role in deciding whether a development project can proceed. Their decisions may, however, be appealed to the state environmental court.

In 2000, Vermont passed another law that was the first of its kind in the nation. It provided that two men or two women living together could form a "civil union" and thus share most of the same legal rights as married couples. In 2009, Vermont lawmakers went a step further and approved a measure allowing gay couples to legally marry. The governor vetoed the measure when it was first passed, but the legislature managed to override his veto by the necessary two-thirds majority. Vermont was the first state to pass such a law.

Who Pays for Schools?

One challenge Vermont lawmakers have faced is the divide between rich towns and poor towns. The state's wealthiest communities, sometimes called "gold

Students examine the original Vermont constitution at the Montpelier statehouse.

towns," include skiing centers such as Stratton and Stowe. Most people in these areas have more money and more-valuable property than citizens in the rest of the state. For a long time, they also had better-funded public schools, because most of the money for schools came from property taxes raised by each town.

In 1997, the Vermont supreme court ruled that students throughout the state should have "substantially equal access" to a good education. In response, the state that year passed the Equal Education Opportunity Act, or Act 60. This law, and a further measure that was passed in 2003, set up a complicated system for funding education in the state. In part it required that residents pay property taxes to the state and that the state, through property tax and other revenues, provide funding for schools equitably.

Taking a Stand

If you live in Vermont and want to get more involved in determining what happens in the state, the first step is learning more. Find out everything you can by reading various newspapers and following the news on the radio, TV, or the Internet. The more you learn about the history of your state and nation and the issues that face people today, the easier it will be to become an informed citizen.

Even if you are not old enough to vote, you can join the political process in Vermont. If you want to support a particular cause or position, try sending an e-mail or a letter to your state senator or representative. Most lawmakers want to be in touch with what ordinary people back home think about the issues of the day. After all, it is these people who may, or may not, vote for them at the next election.

Contacting Lawmakers

★ ★ ★ ★ ★ ★ ★ ★ ★ ★ ★ ★

To contact a member of the Vermont general assembly go to

http://www.leg.state.vt.us/legdir/ findmember3.cfm

Using the map, click on your city or town to find your state representative and state senator. If you prefer to pick your city or town by name, click on the text-only version of the page.

Once you know the name of the senator or representative you need, click on "Legislative Directory" and then look for and click on "Representatives Listed Alphabetically" or "Senators Listed Alphabetically." The list contains the information you need to contact your lawmaker by mail, e-mail, or phone.

Some students in Vermont do vote at election time. They go to the polls with their parents. While the adults use official ballots, the students fill out mock (pretend) ballots. The mock ballots are counted separately, and the results are posted on the Vermont government website. These kinds of programs may encourage students and their families to get involved in the political process.

Sometimes, just connecting with people around you can make a big difference. Students at one elementary school in Westford went door-to-door to find out what their neighbors did for a living. Like many farming areas in Vermont, their community was made up of many small businesses, ranging from producers of maple syrup to designers of websites. The students wrote about what they learned and created a website about the project. By sharing their information, the students helped business owners, who had been working on their own, get to know each other better and cooperate more.

5 Making a Living

Vermont's fresh air, clear water, and scenery make it a great place to live. It can also be a great place to make a living. Like other states, Vermont was hard hit by the nation's economic downturn that began in late 2007. The unemployment rate, which had been under 4 percent, edged up to more than 7 percent by mid-2009. But this was still below the national average, and conditions showed some improvement in 2010 and the beginning of 2011. In spring 2011, the unemployment rate in the Green Mountain State was about 5 percent.

The Vermont economy has strengths in many areas. Some people say the state's economy sits on a three-legged stool, being based on manufacturing, agriculture, and tourism. Both manufacturing and agriculture have indeed contributed to the state's growth. But most of the jobs today are in fields that provide services to people, rather than in the production of goods. Tourism, education, health care, and retail trade are among the most common so-called service industries.

Manufacturing and Mining

Most of Vermont's manufacturing jobs are located near Burlington. Companies in the area make computer chips, software, batteries, and semiconductor equipment. Parts produced in Vermont are needed to make all kinds of electronic

Vermont is home to many professional artists and craftspeople, including glassblowers, potters, and weavers.

BEN AND JERRY

One of the best-known Vermont products is premium ice cream. In 1978, two friends, Ben Cohen and Jerry Greenfield, went into business together so they could be their own bosses—and have fun. They made their own ice cream and sold it in a run-down former gas station in Burlington. Today, people buy their many flavors around the world. As the company grew, Ben and Jerry made sure some of the profits went to causes they believed in. While their ice cream is still a big hit, Ben and Jerry sold the company in 2000 and are no longer involved in running it.

items, from video games to cell phones. The state's high-tech industries have become increasingly important to Vermont's economy.

With its many acres (hectares) of forests, Vermont also remains a center for wood and paper products. Sawmills produce lumber, cabinetmakers build furniture, and printing presses turn out newspapers and business forms. Some companies in the state make equipment for outdoor sports, including snowboards, snowshoes, and fishing rods.

Textile manufacturing declined in the twentieth century as cotton textile factories moved south and synthetic fabrics came into wide use. Machine tools, for use in factories, fared better. Some of the first tools for shaping wood and metal by machine were invented in Windsor in the 1840s. These tools were used to make guns, typewriters, and sewing machines in the state. Today, machine tools made in Vermont help produce paper, steel, cars, and airplanes in factories across the country.

The country's first granite quarry lies just outside Barre, on the eastern side of the Green Mountains. Workers cut big blocks of the rock and haul them to workshops called granite sheds. Some chunks of Vermont granite are carved and polished to make memorial stones. Others are sliced to make the walls of office buildings or cut up for use as kitchen countertops.

Workers & Industries

Industry	Number of People Working in That Industry	Percentage of All Workers Who Are Working in That Industry
Education and health care	86,041	26.5%
Wholesale and retail businesses	48,349	14.9%
Publishing, media, entertainment, hotels, and restaurants	37,009	11.4%
Manufacturing	33,953	10.5%
Professionals, scientists, and managers	28,975	8.9%
Construction	24,205	7.5%
Government	16,007	4.9%
Banking and finance, insurance and real estate	15,065	4.6%
Other services	14,477	4.5%
Transportation and public utilities	11,456	3.5%
Farming, forestry, fishing, and mining	8,930	2.8%
Totals	**324,467**	**100%**

Notes: Figures above do not include people in the armed forces. "Professionals" includes people such as doctors and lawyers. Percentages may not add to 100 because of rounding.

Source: U.S. Bureau of the Census, 2009 estimates

Chunks of marble from Vermont quarries are used to make a variety of high-quality products.

Vermont's marble belt runs through the Taconic Mountains, in the southwestern part of the state. For more than one hundred years, stonecutters in Proctor have been shaping marble columns and graceful monuments. Today, most of this gleaming white stone is ground into a fine powder called calcium carbonate. It is then used to make toothpaste, paint, and plastics.

Living from the Land

Green fields, red barns, and black-and-white cows are a familiar sight in Vermont. Farming is no longer the state's key industry, but even today some seven thousand farms dot the landscape and make an important contribution to the economy. Despite the rocky soil and less-than-ideal climate conditions, Vermont farmers still make a living growing fruits and vegetables, such as apples and potatoes, as well as crops for animal feed, such as hay, corn, oats, and wheat. Some farmers use greenhouses to raise warm-weather produce such as green peppers and tomatoes, as well as nursery plants.

Quick Facts

IT CAME FROM VERMONT
The United Nations Building in New York City is made from Vermont marble. So are the U.S. Supreme Court Building and Jefferson Memorial in Washington, D.C.

Dairy products, however, are the most important farm resource, accounting for two-thirds of all farm revenue. Dairy farms blanket the Champlain Lake valley. Some have been around for more than two hundred years, with the oldest dating back to the American Revolution. At one time, Vermont had more cows than people. Today there are fewer cows, but they actually produce more milk, around 2.5 billion pounds (1.1 billion kg) per year. More than half of it is shipped to other states, while a small amount is sold locally for drinking. The rest goes to make dairy products such as yogurt, butter, ice cream, and more than fifteen kinds of cheese, especially cheddar and mozzarella.

Many farmers earn money from a famous Vermont resource: the sweet sap of the sugar maple tree. They tap the trees by driving a metal spout into the trunk and letting the sap drip into a metal bucket. Pipeline systems are also used to collect the sap. Then, the farmers boil the sap down to make syrup or mouthwatering maple sugar candy. Vermont is the leading maple product producer among the fifty states. Maple products alone account for about 6 percent of the state's farm revenue.

Many Vermonters make maple syrup by tapping trees, collecting the sap in traditional buckets, and boiling it.

RECIPE FOR MAPLE OATMEAL COOKIES

Here is a simple recipe for tasty cookies made with oatmeal and sweet maple syrup.

WHAT YOU NEED

$1/4$ teaspoon (1.5 grams) salt

2 teaspoons (10 g) baking powder

$1 1/4$ cups (100 g) uncooked oatmeal (quick oats)

$1/2$ cup (100 g) shortening

1 egg

$1/4$ cup (40 g) chopped nuts (pecans or walnuts)

1 cup (240 milliliters) maple syrup

$1/2$ teaspoon (2 ml) vanilla extract

$1/4$ cup (60 ml) milk

$1 1/4$ cups (160 g) all-purpose flour

Have an adult help you preheat the oven to 350 °F (175 °C). Combine all the ingredients in a large mixing bowl. Make sure that you mix the batter thoroughly. (With the help of an adult, you can use an electric mixer, on medium speed, if you have one available.)

Lightly grease a cookie sheet. To make each cookie, drop about 1 tablespoon (20 g) of dough on the cookie sheet. Make sure that the cookies are at least $1 1/2$ inches (4 cm) apart.

Bake the cookies for about 10 minutes. (When they are ready, the cookies should be a light brown color.) Carefully remove the cookies and let them cool. Make sure that an adult helps you because the cookie sheet and the baked cookies will be very hot. Once the cookies are cool, enjoy them with a glass of milk.

The Shelburne Museum, near Burlington, houses fine paintings, handcrafted furniture, and many other objects from U.S. history.

Tourism

Millions of visitors travel to Vermont each year, bringing money to the state economy. In summer, people come to hike and camp in untamed areas, such as the Green Mountain National Forest, and to swim, fish, and canoe in sparkling rivers and lakes. In autumn, tourists come especially to enjoy the brilliant fall leaves. Winter brings skiers and snowboarders to mountain resorts such as Stowe, Smugglers' Notch, Killington, and Sugarbush.

Tourists help keep the economy running by staying at hotels, eating in restaurants, and shopping in stores. In addition, many people from outside Vermont have vacation homes in the state. These part-time Vermonters buy property and also pay taxes, giving the state a financial boost.

The outdoors may be Vermont's main tourist attraction, but history and the arts bring people to the state, too. The Shelburne Museum, just south of Burlington, is not just one building, but almost fifty, spread out in a huge park with green lawns and bright flowers. Many of the buildings are more than a century old, including a schoolhouse from 1840 and an inn from 1783. Inside them is one of the largest collections of arts and crafts from America's past.

Milk

Some 135,000 Vermont dairy cows help make milk an important state product. The most common type are black-and-white Holsteins. Each cow can provide more than 6 gallons (23 l) of milk a day.

Apples

The state has some 3,200 acres (1,300 ha) of commercial apple orchards. Crisp Vermont apples are either sold fresh or made into products such as cider, applesauce, and pie. From mid-August through October, families can visit many of the state's orchards and enjoy apple picking together.

Granite

Some of the world's finest granite comes from quarries near Barre, where this stone is an important part of the economy. Vermont ships this heavy building material across the United States and to many other countries.

Electronic Goods

Electronics is Vermont's leading manufacturing industry, and the International Business Machines Corporation, better known as IBM, is the state's biggest employer. The IBM semiconductor plant near Burlington is the biggest industrial plant in the state.

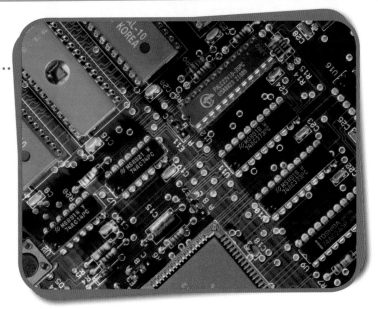

Forests

The acres (ha) of trees that carpet Vermont are used to make everything from lumber to paper to maple syrup. Their fiery fall color brings income to the state by attracting tourists.

Mountains and Snow

Vermont's mountains are a major resource for the tourism industry, attracting hikers, campers, and sightseers. In winter, the snow-covered peaks become a playground for downhill and cross-country skiing, snowboarding, and snowmobiling.

Saving Vermont Farms

Many visitors like to come to Vermont for its simple pleasures. Tourists can drive along a narrow, winding road, pass a two-hundred-year-old covered bridge, buy fresh fruit from a farmer, and then browse in a country store. Vermonters hope the state will be able to keep its old-fashioned charm for years to come. That means protecting the land and preserving historic places. It also means holding on to an important part of the rural way of life: Vermont's farms.

Farming has never been an easy job, and soil and weather conditions in Vermont are tougher than in many other states. Prices can drop so low that farmers earn less money than they need to pay out for feed, equipment, and property taxes. Owners of small farms have an especially hard time. Nowadays some farmers often wind up selling their land to developers, who will pay a high price for the land and use it to build houses or businesses.

Most farmers would rather keep their land if they can still make it profitable, and other people want them to keep it too. "Vermont wouldn't be Vermont without its farmers," says Pam Allen, who grows apples on an old family farm in South Hero. "People here don't want to see parking lots and high-rises. There is no other sight in the world like these apple trees exploding with sweet white blossoms each spring."

Vermonters are doing their best to keep small farms running. One dairy farm in North Ferrisburgh is raising money from investors to start a new milk bottling plant. These farmers are looking for a cheaper way to produce "organic" milk (produced without the use of chemicals) so they can sell it at a good profit. Other farmers are switching to organic crops. People will pay more for organic products,

Farmhouses like this one near Woodstock are an important part of Vermont tradition.

This couple runs an organic dairy farm in Stratford. Organic farming in the state has grown substantially in recent years.

but these also cost more to produce. Some farmers run inns for tourists who are looking to enjoy the experience of life on a farm. Others make and sell specialty foods such as gourmet mushrooms and homestyle jam.

Conservation groups are helping out. The Vermont Land Trust, for example, pays farmers who agree to protect their land from development. Since the group got started in the 1970s, it has saved more than 500,000 acres (200,000 ha) in the state, including 700 working farms. Another organization, the Conservation Law Foundation, is working with the state government to get help for farmers, including tax relief, business advice, and programs to promote products that are grown close to home. One such program, called Vermont Fresh Network, links farmers to restaurants interested in buying their crops.

Farms contribute hundreds of millions of dollars a year to the Vermont economy. They also create the green rolling pastures the state is famous for. Vermonters hope to preserve this valuable asset.

State Flag & Seal

Vermont's flag was adopted in 1923. It displays the state's coat of arms against a blue background. The coat of arms includes a shield with symbols of the state's forests and farms: a pine tree, a cow, bales of hay, and stacks of wheat, with the Green Mountains in the background. The head of a stag, or male deer, is shown at the top of the shield, and pine branches curve around it. The name of the state and Vermont's motto, "Freedom and Unity," appear on a red banner underneath.

The official state seal was created by Ira Allen, an early settler who, like his brother Ethan, helped Vermont become a state. The seal was originally adopted in 1779. It shows the state motto below a pine tree, a cow, sheaves of grain, and wooded hills. A newer version was introduced in 1821, but in 1937, Vermonters decided to return to Ira Allen's original design.

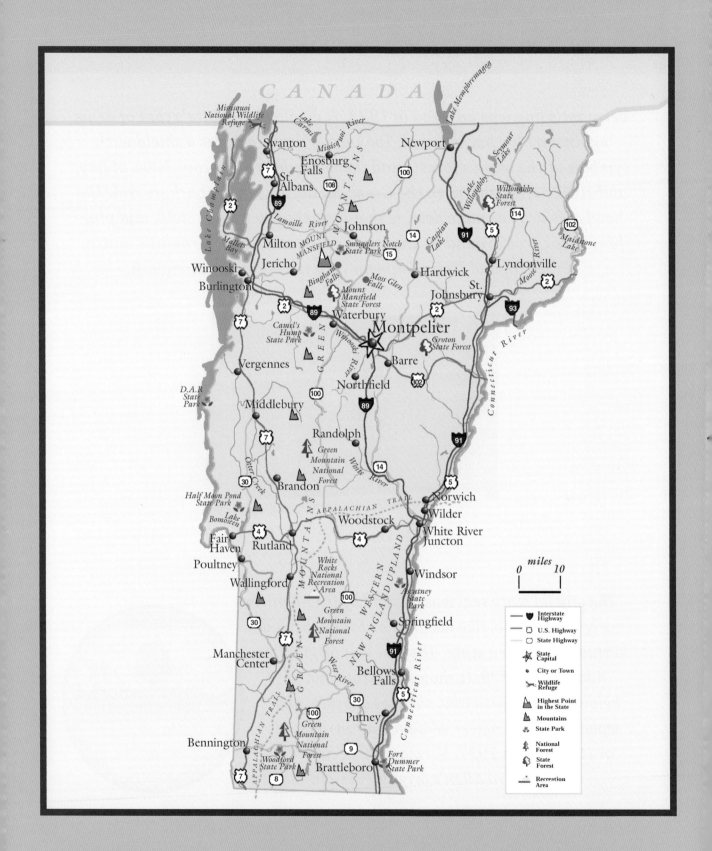

State Song

Hail Vermont!

words and music by Josephine Hovey Perry

BOOKS

Boekhoff, P. M. *Ben and Jerry*. Detroit: KidHaven Press, 2005.

Elish, Dan. *Chester A. Arthur*. Danbury, CT: Children's Press, 2004.

Haugen, Brenda. *Ethan Allen: Green Mountain Rebel*. Minneapolis: Compass Point Books, 2005.

Somers, Michael. *Vermont Past and Present*. New York: Rosen Publishing Group, 2010.

Venezia, Mike. *Calvin Coolidge*. Danbury, CT: Children's Press, 2007.

Wooten, Sarah MacIntosh. *Robert Frost: The Life of America's Poet*. Berkeley Heights, NJ: Enslow Publishers, 2006.

WEBSITES

Official State of Vermont Tourism Site:
http://www.travel-vermont.com

Official State of Vermont Website:
http://www.vermont.gov

Vermont Fish and Wildlife Department:
http://www.vtfishandwildlife.com

Vermont Secretary of State Kids Pages:
http://www.sec.state.vt.us/Kids

Margaret Dornfeld is a writer, editor, and translator in New York City. She loves painting, cooking, and listening to Latin music. On summer days, she likes to escape the city and go canoeing in the lakes and rivers of Vermont.

William McGeveran, as editorial director at World Almanac Books, developed many editions of *The World Almanac and Book of Facts* and *The World Almanac for Kids*. Now a freelance editor and writer, he has four children who are grown up and four grandchildren who will soon be old enough to read this book.

Page numbers in **boldface** are illustrations.